Staring Directly at the Eclipse

New and Selected Poems

Henry Normal

*Dedicated to my wife Angela
and my son Johnny.*

You are the shape of my world.

Staring Directly at the Eclipse

New and Selected Poems
Henry Normal

Five Leaves Publications
www.fiveleaves.co.uk

Staring Directly at the Eclipse
Henry Normal

Published in 2016 by Five Leaves,
14a Long Row, Nottingham NG1 2DH

www.fiveleaves.co.uk
www.fiveleavesbookshop.co.uk

ISBN 978-1-910170-40-3

Cover illustration by
Johnny Carroll-Pell

Typeset and designed by
Four Sheets Design and Print

Printed in Great Britain

Contents

ACKNOWLEDGEMENTS

I'd like to thank Colette Bryce, Matt Welton, Linda Hallam, Penny Shepperd and Ross Bradshaw for their help in bringing this collection together.

The Breath within the Balloon

The breath within the balloon will not last
You never get inflated balloons
on the Antiques Road Show
Breath brings with it vulnerability

If never inflated
a balloon may last forever
but such limp reason
will never enchant a child
with decoration
or gladden the heart
with the stretching of possibility
and the fulfilment of promise

Is not a universe of such balloons sadder
than a universe where balloons are apt to burst?

I hold your breath within my hands

The breath within the balloon will not last
but the giving of breath
and the tying of the knot
at each new birth
is an offering
for our choice of worlds

If Signatures Reflect Personality
They Cannot All Remain Constant

It's not that I've forgotten my own name
it's just that my signature doesn't flow naturally like it
    used to

I hesitate as the pen blotches the first ink, self-conscious
Each letter has become foreign, a random code of symbols

With deliberate forgery I have to match up my
    commitment with a
genuine signature that has already been approved

I'm cribbing off my own past

It's as if my signature is trying to change but is
    restrained
by the functional need of the authorised version

Strange how we set our own guidelines, our own
    parameters
so early for something so permanent

I remember practising my signature as a teenager
I'm sure I never understood this was to remain
unchanged forever

As a result my signatures have become clumsy
like a child's crayon letters

I suppose I'm worried if I just sign a new signature
this will not be accepted

Is it possible to authorise a change of signature?
How will I sign for it?

I am Not Belittled
by Your Culture of Ambition

My wife has a moustache
It is plastic
It came out of a Christmas cracker

We are monarchy
in our paper hats

I am King Superman in his favourite cardigan
full of pud

It's not a thought-through image
we are ramshackle
a homely mess
like bric-a-brac
at a car boot

There is no sleekness to our design
no colour co-ordination
no concession to taste

Against all rules of fashion
and all aesthetic consideration
we are happy
at ease
daft in love

There Is Love at First Sight

There is wonder in attraction
the dancing of light on the retina
the alignment of atoms into form and substance
the perception of science as nature

Anatomy and biology raised to aesthetics and beauty
the tautness of flesh over muscle and frame
the way fabric clings to an outline
the contours of a rib cage
the tilt of a pelvis
the enticement of hollows and shadows
poise and the grace of texture

Colours and tones that blend and sculpt the imagination
the vulnerability of a neckline
the fragrance of moisture and the lure of intoxication
the glow of touch and the genius of the blood's energy
there is miracle in personality
there is wonder in attraction
there is love at first sight
I am already yours

The House Is Not the Same since You Left

The house is not the same since you left
the cooker is angry – it blames me
The tv tries desperately to stay busy
but occasionally I catch it staring out of the window
The washing up's feeling sorry for itself again
it just sits there saying "What's the point, what's the point?"
The curtains count the days
Nothing in the house will talk to me
I think your armchair's dead
The kettle tried to comfort me at first
but you know what its attention span's like
I've not told the plants yet
they still think you're on holiday
The bathroom misses you
I hardly see it these days
it still can't believe you didn't take it with you
The bedroom won't even look at me
since you left it keeps its eyes closed
all it wants to do is sleep, remembering better times
trying to lose itself in dreams
it seems like it's taken the easy way out
but at night I hear the pillows
weeping into the sheets

The Missing Page

and it made a mockery of the rest

and it became the most important of all pages

and neither of us could write a replacement

and we could never agree on its contents
        only sometimes in broad outline

and there were times when we denied it had ever existed
and times when I believed it to be several pages

and it became the perfect excuse

and the amount we attributed to it could never be
contained on

                                        a single

sheet

and if only the pages had never been numbered

and

The Last Parents

Huddled around
the very last sun
a final handful of humans
try yet again to create
one artificial star that will survive

The parents telling that same story
of how the sky once dazzled with a million suns

How
as
one by one the lights went out
generation after generation
traced a path like a dot-to-dot
to this
the final glimmer

And how once there were as many souls
in the universe as there were these stars

And how their parents had told them
this story when they were young

And how their parents had told them
not to be afraid of the dark

A Prayer for the Rejected

We start from nothing and build
and you may
judge down from perfection

catalogue all that we are not
measure against legends and eons
ignore mitigation

dismiss originality as untested
discard hand-crafted as unprofessional
destroy with a whim

discount our unborn
belittle our dreams
and despite all this

again
we start from nothing and build

Skin

More skin than I could possibly need
has been arriving at my door now for weeks
There is no return address

I've tried giving it away to friends
but they have no use for it

I've taken out ads in the local paper
I've even tried car boot sales
but there seems to be a glut in the market at the moment

I had a word with the Post Office
but there's nothing they can do

I'm running out of storage space
I can no longer get my car in the garage

I've secretly tried dumping bin bags full at night
but I swear the same skin arrives back in the morning
together with the standard delivery

In desperation I burnt several layers in the back garden
but the neighbours complained
and a man from the Council called round and said
I was causing a health risk

I'm resigned to carrying as much as I can about with me now
It's all I can think to do

I can see people staring at me
pitying me
whispering behind my back
asking if I can breathe under all that skin

I could post the skin onto someone else
like a chain letter
but I wouldn't wish this on anyone

The Frame of the Mona Lisa Dreams

Though you have looked in my direction many times
you do not remember me
Hung on a wall on my own
you would not exalt me

I have intrinsic value

but this notoriety is not of my own making
I have seen eyes filled with wonder glance over me

Like the plain sister
I see all
but am not seen
The curious and the cynical I see
the desperate and the disappointed

Like the assassin my fame is a reflection
like the bodyguard I am expendable
I know my place at court

And in all the borrowed light shined upon me
from my vantage at the edge of the glare
occasionally I see refracted
in the tiring of a gaze
something of myself

A gentle sob
almost, yet not quite, lost

Remember me
it seems to say

Remember me
and I will remember you

Photos with My Son

Johnny is not interested in having his
photo taken

When prompted he will look at the lens
His hand is likely to move at any moment

I suspect he is not sure what is expected of him
'Smile,' he says

He doesn't smile
he just says smile

echoing the words
from behind the camera

Summer on Pluto

In a room with no windows
I am given a leaflet

The word incurable
is printed in bold on the first page

This is the only time I will spend in this room
This is the only time I will speak to this person

Autism is a spectrum
there are degrees

Your son is mildly severe
What does that mean?

It means he will always live at home
it means he will never have a job

never have a girlfriend
never be capable of taking care of himself

You will never have a conversation with him
ever

It means you will worry about him every day
you will worry if he's happy

you will worry if he's lonely
you will worry what will happen to him when you die

Mildly severe
benignly savage

kindly cruel
none of this appeared on the leaflet

Logic Is Not a Feeling

The horizon out to sea
feels like the nearest nature gets to
a straight line

Seen from any one coast
the curve is slight

There is comfort
in the simplicity
of such a vast uninterrupted skyline

Something peaceful
in the lack of clutter

With a cloudless sky
and very little wave
the meeting of the light and royal blue
is perfection

You can be forgiven
for thinking that if you go beyond this reach
you fall

adrift without compass

The Eating of a Unicorn

So I'm eating this unicorn and I'm thinking
this isn't right
but you've got to eat, haven't you?

So you tell yourself it's OK
everybody eats them
but you know that's not strictly true

So you look for some justification, some strand of logic
some attitude, some philosophy, however slim
but you know in your gut it still isn't right

So you think about minimising the damage
but you know you can't simply throw up and piece the whole
business back together

So you say what is done is done and you have to live with
it
but you still wish you hadn't eaten the bloody thing
and wonder how you could have ever felt that hungry

So you pretend it never happened
that you know nothing about it
and besides, you thought it was just a horse made up

But now you have to dispose of what's left of the body
and in case it's discovered
you have to hide the head and the horn separately

So there you are, breaking off the head and the horn
from a half eaten unicorn at dead of night
but

King Canute Should
Have Checked the Tides

Taking your own chair to the beach
is a commitment
fleecy on
hood up

Better to keep your limbs moving
some might say

but sitting is a definite statement
We are not just passing through
we are making a stand
sitting firm

Day trippers we are not
nor ill-prepared tourists
We are stones amongst scattered pebbles
rocks amongst shingle

Bring on your highest wave
the glory is ours
we live here
we own this weather

The First Spark Has Led to This Blaze

All stories are universal
All told from a unique point of view

This is the universe
at this moment
from this perspective

Whether you want to or not
you represent life

You are what life looks like
at this instant
from this vantage
from inside the vast array

The story of life
the story of creation witnessed
from the first spark
to the disintegration of the very last cell
is one story
our story

Whether you are interested enough
to engage or not
or brave enough
to contribute further
you are already part of the narrative

At this pulse
from a collusion of all that has gone before
you are life
you are the universe

you are the story

Animals and Small Children Find Me Out

It is not that I am of no worth
just that I've managed to exaggerate my worth

or at least I've allowed my worth to be exaggerated
beyond my ability to pretend justification

Animals and small children find me out

I don't even keep plants around the house nowadays
I had hoped to live up to this flattery

but it becomes a chore
like constantly walking around on tiptoes

and sooner or later you wonder
at the true benefit of the extra height

The Perfect You

I am the other you
the perfect you
the one bred from your DNA
taken at birth
our birth
cultivated for spare parts
kept alive by machines

We grow simultaneous
alike but not quite
for I have no defects
no scars
no scratches
no weathered skin
no blemishes
no bruises
no acquired resistance
no yellowing of the eye
no tooth decay
no furrows in the brow
no creases on the palms

no lifeline
no loveline

I am the other you
the perfect you
stored in the dark
waiting

Cueva de las Manos

I place my left hand
on that most solid

Spread out my fingers
to form a stencil

Blow kaolin and manganese
through hollow bone
to leave a silhouette

Whether we call it art
or human nature

on every continent
something survives

vulnerable as dust

Over two thousand generations call
each with a simple statement
as urgent as blood through veins

I am here
I am here
I am here

Abiogenesis to Revelations

Twenty watts amid all this vitality

My one descendant
holds a dinosaur up to the sunset
We are engaged in an exchange of energy

Half the stars in the Milky Way
shine inside this precious three pounds

Electromagnetic radiation hitting the retina
fires the optic nerve
with the enormity of creation

The alchemy of emotion overwhelms
The ache infinite

I'm told
there are no numbers or names in nature
existence is independent of the mind

love and beauty
just icons on a computer screen

I am overawed by every single atom
Moments like this I could believe in God
Moments like this I could kiss him

The Joy of Frogs

Frogs need kisses like anyone else

Not all of them want to become handsome princes
some prefer a more pond-based lifestyle

What if you turn into a handsome prince and the princess
really
prefers frogs?

What if you're not that handsome a prince?
Maybe you're more handsome a frog?

Let's face it, chances are
if you can get kissed fairly regularly by a princess
and remain a frog
you've got it made

If she gives you tongues
then go for it

Beauty and the Insect Heart

The ocean is the wisest of counsellors
Before its double moon
comforted by a mother's breath
I offer my heart as a small gift of stones

This is the closest I may get to perfection
I saw a thousand shoes today but one pair of eyes
They've discovered over a million stars
but so far only one planet with life

Some distance along the shore line
I can see a young couple
They are easy and familiar
They have something
all my sullen romance cannot reach

There is no urgency now
only the hurting of a single truth

I would give everything, everything
to share such acceptance
Not just with anyone, not just in abstract
but vivid like the cleansing of pain
or the healing of fractured bone

Here I will soothe the night
Here I will help build a cathedral of words

not for worship or inanimate passion
or another broken relic on a forgotten mound
but for someone, someone close, knelt alone
somewhere on a distant beach
offering her heart as a small gift of stones

Later, nursing the motorway north and home
the sunrise whispers promises in a rear view mirror

A Gift

At 7 o'clock this morning
I bring you a mountain,
I tap gently on your window
and you wake half covered in sleep

"What's that?" you ask
"It's a mountain" I grin
"I've carried it all night
I couldn't sleep so I brought it here to show you"

"What do I want with a mountain in my garden
at 7 o'clock in the morning?" you ask
not used to being woken at 7 o'clock
with a mountain in your garden

I try to joke, now feeling a little embarrassed

"It's for you, a gift"
You say you don't want a mountain
You are too tired to understand
and I struggle to explain

it's not the mountain I've brought you
it's the fact that I could bring it to you
I strain to pick it up again
and wonder what I'm going to do with it now

I feel such a fool walking home with a mountain

If You Should Ever Climb a Tree

I'm not sure how much weight
my head can support

but I enjoy the familiarity
the casual lack of boundaries

Without a word
we get a sense of someone

If you should ever climb a tree
I will be your low hanging branch
I want that to be unquestioned

If my neck snaps
it was meant to be

It is the most important thing
to know

In the absence of sufficient language
I would rather seek out trees
to remind you

Uncomfortably Positive

This might not seem that different a picture to you
but this is the look of a mother
to her autistic child
taking his first photo

The look of a mother
anticipating success

the coal face of optimism
the body language of hope

If I was susceptible to joy
this could easily affect me

Unlike my wife
I have immunity
to all forms of jubilation

I err towards caution
bordering scepticism
on matters of good fortune or progress

This condition we embrace
I've learnt is not linear
not predictable like neurotypical behaviour

Five minutes after you leave us
you will turn to one another and say
'Well, we can see where that comes from'

She Is Not Looking at the Camera

She is not looking at the camera
What can she see?
There's something off
a thought, a memory
There's a hint of a smile
but a faraway sadness in her eyes

Am I projecting
or sensitive to disparity?
Singling out the one expression amid the group
disregarding the set instruction
There is the suspicion of sea in the distance
All detail of sky is lost in monochrome

Heavy clothes suggest
the weather is bracing
but these were the days of formality
even on the promenade
Where are you?
yours is the thought that intrigues me

It's easy to look into the camera
It's what is expected
Isn't the unexpected more interesting though?
somehow more beautiful
more human
a quiet blow for a world of other

The Questions They
Don't Ask on the Census

Hands up anyone
who is lonely
or has ever felt loneliness?

Anyone who has hidden themselves away
on New Year's Eve
rather than face that hiatus
of emptiness in public?

Anyone who has dressed up
on a Saturday night
and forced themselves out
into the melee
only to return home
having not spoken to a single soul?

Anyone who has searched faces on the pavement
for a fragment of recognition?

Anyone who has stood at the edge of a window in hope?

Anyone who has touched a photo in remembrance?

Anyone who has put a pillow behind them in the dark
against the cold?

Anyone who finds a mirror the hardest place to look
or lowers their eyes when they meet someone?

Anyone who aches without knowing what for?
Anyone afraid of being found wanting?

Should Tenderness Become Plague

Should tenderness become plague
glory in its infection
carry its contagion
and pray the germ is hereditary

Staring Directly at the Eclipse

Your feet on my lap
as we settle for the night

A shoreline to ourselves
Sunlight on water

Nature catching the eye unexpected
Fresh air intoxicating

Getting lost in art or endeavour
Music that carries and caresses

Food presented as a gift
Being surprised by genius or kindness

Your face flush and immediate
A friendly soul at my window

Hope in all forms however tiny
The comforting mundanity of doing nothing much

The absence of pain and fear
however fleeting

A familiar arm around my shoulder
The satisfaction of something done well

Loyalty and honour embraced
Minor revelations of perception

The defiance of spirit against overwhelming odds
Valour and grace in the face of the inevitable

To spite death
and make his victory hollow

Is Memory Thought or Emotion?

Monkey bin
is a huge monkey head on a bin

It's not a real monkey
it doesn't move or make a noise
it has no arms or legs or body
just a head on top of a waste bin

This is Johnny's favourite bit of the zoo
Mine too

Johnny did like the penguins
It's a relief to know what he likes
or doesn't like
it's probably the basis of all
personality

He hates erratic noise
dogs and babies or
young girls who can't get what they want

I was drawn to the infant giraffes
awkward and strangely poetic
Johnny wasn't impressed
the moment came and went

The tiger intimidated
I could see in his eyes
he'd fuck me up if he could

I'm sure there were other animals
real monkeys and shit

but the only animals I remember
apart from monkey bin

are the giraffes, the tiger and
the penguins
and what I felt when I saw them

It's more the feeling I recall
and a yearning
for connection

Beauty without Numbers

Presented with Colour By Numbers
he chooses only what colour he wants
only what borders appeal

The figurative made abstract
The shape of the world embellished

New edges imagined
The pallet reinvigorated

A choice is braved
A universe decided
Personality shaming mathematics

Lines enhanced as never before
to create
a map of self-determination

This Is Not a House of War

Everything I want for my children
I want for your children

Everything I wish for me
I wish for you

This is not a house of fear
This is a house of life

How can I not see myself in you
If you look
how can you not see yourself in me

You are respected as much as I am
You are of worth in equal measure

You are family
You are us

This is not a house of intolerance
This is a house of acceptance

We are the house
You and I

This is where you belong
This is where we belong

This is your home
This is our home

Flux Could Kill

Two feet from certain death
Two feet of existence
not menacing but matter of fact
The choice is always as narrow as this
only here
you can measure spirit

The grass leans outward
The cliff
jagged with purpose
penetrates the waves

Two feet of lies and soft options
Two feet of fear and pulse
There is a truth that's too easy to forget until you fill your
lungs with determination

At times such as dusk
there is wonder in the commonplace

Rain hangs on the skyline
Beauty is always this short a distance

I have spent my whole life trying to enter the gates of
heaven
using my heart as a battering ram

Two feet of the attainable
Two feet from acceptance

As If We Could Bottle This
and Take It with Us

We travel as far as the Romans
to recreate home

A simple meal
elegance without formality

Trees surround our table
like the quietest of staff

There is a scent of eucalyptus
a distant fountain underscores

Early afternoon
softened by leaves

The world is busy elsewhere
scorpions on an open fire

Nature pays us no mind
we breathe our own space

We bathe in the spring
and dance on hand paved stone

We are invisible
to all but ourselves

Sex and the Kissing of Salt

The rhapsody of gesture
a covenant of nature

a merging of fluids and gentleness
the homage of caress

the warmest gift
a mutual worship

the applauding of skin
the salutation within

the sincerest poetry
the perfect society

the reverence of the body's grace
the innermost embrace

the enchantment of response
the harmony of imbalance

the threshold of adoration
the theatre of captivation

a more intimate fame
the empathy bargain

the exaltation of the senses
the camaraderie of indulgences

the ballad of creation
the divine celebration
the glory of immersion

The Dream Ticket

Man with obvious disability in maintaining relationships seeks all-consuming passion but will settle for friendship and the occasional shag. Doesn't believe relationships ever work but has been known to fake undue optimism.

Woman must be classic beauty, half saint half whore (ONO). Must be 100 per cent loyal but tolerant of bumbling indiscretion. Must have no friends that she wouldn't ditch just to spend a few extra seconds in my presence.

Must be available to lavish attention on me whenever I need pampering but have interesting things to do when I'm busy so that I can be entertained when we next meet.

Must have no friends that are male, unless they are grossly ugly. All female friends should be incredibly horny and desperate to sleep with me given the slightest chance.

Must be caring and gentle in bed but willing to be ravished, tied up and have various substances smeared over specific portions of the anatomy. Must cum very loudly every time we have sex. Must synchronise with each of my orgasms. Must groan and moan softly until the final stages then shout such comments as 'I've never had it so good', 'You're so big' and 'God, I love you'.

Must burst into tears for no reason occasionally and when challenged say, 'I don't want to lose you'.

Must hate every one of my male friends. Find them sexually repulsive and inferior to me in every way. Must understand that my female friends are just friends and that's different.

Must always have a worse time than me at parties. Must hate parties, students, arty wankers, wanky art students, parties with wanky art students.

Must be completely naive, innocent and optimistic but worldly wise. Must be young at heart but sensible. Must be practically a virgin but have a sophisticated knowledge of sexual technique.

Must be intelligent but not so that it makes me realise my simplistic thought processes.

Most importantly must realise that all the above is not a joke.

Please send tasteful nude photo.

Saving Me from the Monotone

I have no qualifications
no legitimacy
no foundation
I do have a chunky computer

I am dressing down
industrial

I am trying
I am trying to be serious
I am trying hard to be serious
I am trying too hard to be serious
like the metallic grey bricks behind us

You are smiling
leaning into me
but in reality
I am leaning into you

Telegraph Poles and Ships' Masts

Telegraph poles and ships' masts
are hard to tell apart
from a distance

We are sitting on a wall
by the harbour

With my golfing hat on
you can't see the onset of grey
or tell that I don't play golf

With Johnny's arm around his mum
you might not tell he's autistic
even at 17

Although the wooden Pinocchio
he holds to his face
might make you question

If you look closely telegraph poles
are connected
whereas ships' masts aren't

as ships sail away in different directions

A Bed Made into a City
Sightseeing Tour Bus

On your left you will see
a boy who only plays with adults

Though he's sitting in the driving seat
he has his back to the steering wheel

Teddy bears are passengers
the wheels are paper plates

Someone has gone to a bit of trouble

But the bus is only visible from the outside
Inside it requires imagination

or the retention of the view from the outside
or is the little boy just sitting in his bed

behind a hand-made barrier?

Night Fishing

You can choose to give these mountains
any name you want
at this moment they are yours

To the north
                no sign of human habitation
untamed ridges muted blue and grey
backlit with a peach haze

To the east
                a line of street lights
marks out civilisation
like a landing strip

To the south
                across the plasma screen
of the lake's surface
beacons appear on the slopes
and reflect
like the tracks of tears

To the west
                the lap of the wake
a moored yacht sways so gently
as if to lull a baby to sleep

At the heart
                in a small rowboat
a man and his son
sit and fish
in water from the ice age
silent as a distant star

We are greater than Gods tonight
we are life

Tinned Fruit and Evaporated Milk

So it was last Saturday tea time when I called in at my dad's
He was sat checking his racing results
I ambled across the room and turned off the TV

'Just a second,' I said tentatively before he started to protest
'I've got something important to tell you'

I hesitated a moment, then bracing myself I came right out
with it
 'I love you dad'

'Don't be so bloody daft', he said

'It's not daft', I said 'I love you'

'Err....alright put kettle on then', he said

'No, you're supposed to say — I love you too son — c'mon dad
you've seen Dallas'

'I've not got time for all this bloody nonsense, I'm off to the
Legion', he said

So I'm following him down the garden and I'm saying
'look dad, I'm in my fifties now and I think it's about time it
was out in the open
I love you'

And he's trying to shh me in case the neighbours hear

So I shout louder, 'I don't care if the whole world hears,
I'm not ashamed of my feelings, I love you, you're my dad'
And I give him a big wet kiss on the forehead
'What do you say dad, what do you say?'

'Oh Henry', he said 'Where did I go wrong?'

When Words are Not Your First Language

Any parent would sooner be ill
than their child

There is a helplessness

Johnny can't quite get the hang
of blowing his nose

His top lip gets raw
like bacon hitting the pan
I wince
and close my eyes to steel myself

Strangely he allows
more contact when poorly
he loses his edges
his lovableness is irresistible

Patience and distraction
are the only prescription

His mum throws her heart
into bamboozling him
through the worst

with such attention and diversion
we could call it just an everyday devotion

There are no words for what passes here

The Sleeping Giant

You lift your face to the open sky
and lie with the sediment
where the sea and stones have come to an accord

And you wonder how you couldn't have
known about this place before

It existed before
and you existed
and now you are aware

And this could be your favourite place
as though the elements had conspired
to fashion and fit your shape

And to think you almost didn't turn that corner
that you had become tired of corners

doubted their promise

And suddenly a world of corners surprises
presents possibility
adventure
illumination
hope

Sand between the Toes

This is what constitutes an action shot in my world

The thinning at my crown is conveniently out of frame
The avalanche under my chin obscured

If I have a best side, this is it

According to my father-in-law's socks it's Monday
The mid-west easiness to his attire betrays no irony
other than that he's from Peterborough

Johnny shows the least interest in having his feet cleaned
he'd make a good pharaoh
nonchalant during de-sanding
ear defenders and fiddly bit of plastic now part of the ensemble

I use his red sock like a shoe-shine boy
buffing the digits

My mother-in-law relaxes leaning forward
her walking sticks hook the bench
like stabilisers

Autistic Family Robinson

Even behind a camera my wife is the centre

If she dies first
we will be buried alive in her tomb
we just don't know it yet

Hidden Chestnut at Herstmonceux

Outliving the royal houses of Europe
sweetness, cultivated by humans

We are children beneath your branches
paying tribute

We've returned to stand at your root
and let you know you are not forgotten

As generations have passed
there is no footfall here
but explorers and pilgrims

Though we only stop a while
sought with affection
favourites are understood

The decades are long
the seconds too short

We are holding up
seeing old friends
sharing time with family

An Acceptable Use of an Exclamation Mark

Johnny looks good in a hat
not self-conscious

I'm always wondering if I should
take a hat off when I go indoors

Johnny is definite
if he's keeping it on, that's it

I'm guessing he's deciding what he wants
not what you think about it

He came over to me
yesterday

and put his arm around my shoulder
for a second

Then he said
'Daddy to go'

I said
'You came over to me!'

but those are my rules
not his

The Jar of Joy

No amount of sugar can preserve it
A euphoric surge unscheduled unable to sustain

Freak weather within the soul
A guest that's always welcome but seldom turns up

Giving back control to the cosmos
for but a breath

Unsettled by an overwhelming gratitude for being
Momentarily in love with the whole bloody mess

The perfect wave in a restless surf
A sudden realisation of possibility

Optimism made tangible for an instant
A fresh breeze through an open heart

Beach of Light

Surveying the sand sculptures on Luz Beach
I'm reminded of Ozymandias, King of Kings
Look on my works, ye Mighty and despair!

There is a two foot pyramid, a hippo and a child-friendly T-rex
an over-sized snail and other animals I can't quite make out
Johnny drops a euro into the man's hat but from such a height
it could easily be mistaken for attitude

We share the tide with a starfish
The moon finds its way through cloud

Balancing on a rock
Lifting one leg at a time
We toy with gravity and its eventual victory

I straighten my back
Lift my head as high as I can
Not yet you've got me, not yet

The Wish List

To arrive at a place
where the past has no pain

where frailty is accepted

where all is beauty
immediate, important
connected, indivisible
exquisite

The greatest show in the universe
and you with a front seat
and you are the star

and everything is Life
and Life is everything
and you are Life
and you are everything

To arrive at a place
where all is cherished
and you are cherished
and you
cherish yourself
and breathe

and breathe

Gravestones at a Wedding

Before God
we are outsiders on the edge

We can appear to fit in
until you look closely

My watch hangs from my wrist
My wife's dress displays birds in flight

My boy leans against the cold stone
head down

We are not really here
or we're too here

Awkward
self-conscious

Not knowing the rules
not understanding what is expected of us

Mirroring, echoing
not knowing where our edges are

Hesitant ghosts
checking our invitations

Windmills amongst Almonds and Oranges

Trees stripped of cork cover the slopes
straggling the crest like
stray hairs on the back of an old man's neck

Alien on hills of metallic blue
a giant Tai Chi class
waves in greeting

Stood in cool formation
like a Reservoir Dogs poster
windmills amongst almonds and oranges

These sleek prefects lord it
with a serene semaphore
nobility in the mist

Such synchronised grace reminds me of
pensioners moving in the edges of the sea

Photo Bombing God

A palm is four fingers
A foot is four palms
A cubit is six palms
Four cubits make a man

My son's skin is almost prepubescent perfect
sideburns suggesting maturity awaits

From the sacred to the unanchored
a sequence of genes mutate

geometry
is remapped

I'm resigned to the thinning of grey
a turning stubble hides my scars

Johnny is far cooler in his sunglasses
he wears a straw hat with the ease of a teenager

Nucleic acid replaces architectural design
twenty-three chromosome pairs roll

I've shaved my eyebrow in the middle
so as not to resemble a Neanderthal

We are a little burnt by the sun
I can't believe my face was once as small as his

The Tree of Life twists in a double helix
the canon of proportions spiral

I look into the camera because I know it's expected
and one of us has to

Johnny still displays no compulsion to conform
he has no interest in consequence

Two thousand two hundred hopes disorder
The Archangel's detail is without error

A pace is four cubits
A man is twenty-four palms
A man is twenty thousand five hundred proteins coding
A man is three billion pairs of chance

The Ulterior Motivator

I've looked for you
all my adult life

in the proudest of my achievements
in the embarrassment of my shortcomings

in the possibilities of every relationship
in the eye contact of every stranger

in the opening of every door
from the window of every train
on every horizon out to sea

in loud and smoke-filled rooms
over the rim of every glass

across every public gathering
down the line of every queue

in the glare of every headlight
in every face of every crowd

in the most bleak of landscapes
in the closing of every curtain

I've looked for you

A Kind of Loving

She came home one day and he'd gone
In his favourite chair he'd left a yoghurt
Unaccustomed to change
she lived with the yoghurt for three years
It never moved from the chair
They slept apart
She often wondered if there was someone else
It never ate what she served up
It ignored relatives
She would often have to hoover round it
Her sister in law told her she was barmy
to stick it out this long
But she knew that marriage was something you had to
work at
She went to marriage guidance on her own
until they said they could do nothing further
if the yoghurt didn't accompany her on
the next visit
Eventually she packed her bags and left
It was a hard decision
You can't live with a yoghurt for three years
without it leaving its mark on your life
She had some fond memories though
of those early days,
and kept a photo of the yoghurt amongst her letters.

The Fisherman of Alvor

There is a dinosaur
unconcerned by our presence

He is waiting upon his prey
black wings outstretched for balance
patient as the grim reaper

His reflection in the water is an anchor
the inlet gunmetal grey
ripples iron filings

Loaded clouds move like tectonic plates
I am sitting with your mother, unsteady

We are temporary
Vulnerable

Too human to settle in this chill landscape
we walk a little to warm the blood

A View to Die For

If this balcony collapses I am extinct

but it is a risk I take casually
this ageless vista is essential
to a life wholly lived

When my wife and son join me
I am a little more conscious of odds
and consequences

When he starts banging the side
I begin to feel increasingly mortal
the scenery becoming less vital with each blow

An Offering to the People of the Mounds

I am wearing hand-me-downs from my son
at the edge of these white cliffs
where the grass is at its greenest

We are an army of one
three heads
six arms
strong in faith and valour

Our passion is unrecorded
in the book of invasions

Our small rebellion
may not be legend

but imagination is the greatest freedom
and no matter how poor
you can always afford ancestors

I wave farewell
from Niall of the nine hostages
from the crossbowman on the battlements
from the sons on Mil Espaine

We are here amongst the cormorants
we have reached this isle of destiny
we are the Angel of the South

Poetry is all around us and within us
This is a land of abundance
as holy as we believe

Lost amid the cloud
descendant of the High Kings

The Couple Next Door —
a Sharing Experience

The couple in the flat next door are always considerate enough to save their arguments until it's time for bed.

This selfless gesture ensures that their intimate secrets, their sexual inadequacies, inferiority and persecution complexes, petty jealousies, childhood traumas, parental rejections, adolescent failings, perverse lust fantasies, unfulfilled animal needs, and their constant insecurity in the other's commitment to the relationship are all that much easier for us to enjoy.

The annoying thing is though that he insists on whimpering in a weak pathetic whine that's very difficult to make out. She on the other hand has perfect diction through a rising scale from full pitch screaming right up to violent hysterical frenzy, at which she is particularly entertaining. It seems a general rule for both that the logic content of the argument decreases in direct proportion to the volume and speed of delivery. Another annoying habit he has is that of speaking away from the adjoining wall and I get the feeling sometimes that he's a little embarrassed at what he's actually saying. She however grasps every opportunity to exploit this weakness and gain the upper hand by repeating his sentences word for word in the form of a very loud exclamation.

A problem they share jointly is the frequent compulsion to storm off into another room after a particularly good line. Other distractions include the unnecessarily long pauses often mistaken for a premature aborting of the conflict leaving both participants and audience alike with a frustrating sense of anti-climax, and the sporadic fits of door banging that can so often surprise even the most careful of listeners, causing any glass not firmly held to make that embarrassing smashing sound as it drops from your ear to the foot of the wall.

Possibly the most pitifully pathetic and therefore the most interesting phase of the argument usually comes when he's ready to make up but she's not quite ready. For the next six or seven minutes he's apologetic and condescending, then after one too many rejections he suddenly blows his top stomping around and shouting such memorable classics as, "I'm trying to be nice to you, you stupid prat!"

I don't think he's actually ever hit her though she's been violent, often unnervingly violent, many times, but once I understand in desperation trying to disperse the anger he spat full in her face. You could tell from the immediate reaction that he knew even as it happened it was the worst thing he could do. Listening to two broken people crying in the night can suddenly make you feel very lonely. At this point I usually hug my girlfriend tight and thank God that tonight the argument was next door.

The Garden Is Still There Underneath

Red trousers draw the eye
like blood on the snow
or stigmata on a holy shroud

It's hard in the wide shot
to tell who is present

We are rolling winter
My hands are stinging
my son's must be

White is the predominant colour
dark green and brown compete with black
like a stencil

Bleak but with majesty
this is our world
this is us
We are where we belong

Even in the coldest of breath
we have our own beauty
it doesn't shout
it is noise-intolerant

Those footprints in the snow
they are ours

Vanguard of Audacious

Kindness is bravery at its brazen best
Its boldest and most ballsy

It empowers all it touches

To put your heart in the line of fire
Is as heroic as it is honourable

To be gentle you offer up a vulnerable underbelly
Empathy and humanity are gifts that entail risk

No matter how everyday it may seem
To dare to act not in self-interest
Is valiant

To demand dignity for others undaunted is intrepid

To find strength to confront and challenge prejudice
requires courage
However uncool to cynics

To make a stand for justice, equality and even love
Is never unfashionable, never untimely

To insist that tenderness endures and that mercy is
victorious
You put your body above the parapet

To face injury, loss, ridicule or one of a hundred fears
But still have resolve and compassion
Is a testament to an indomitable spirit

On whatever scale
The matter-of-factness of such nobility
Is a quiet but magnificent defiance

The Heart of the Last Mammoth

Not even on prime time TV
but on the minority interest channel
I saw a scientist break open the heart of a mammoth
'It is very rare,' he said
'There are only two in existence'

We were never told if
the other mammoth's heart
had yet been broken

Does a Bad Curtain Call Ruin a Show?

I'm never any good at goodbyes

I feel too much pressure
to produce some sort of fitting climax
As though fulfilling a duty or observing the
constraints of an art form

It's the unalterable finality
I feel looming like a punchline
you know is not going to work

A polite thank you and goodnight
never seems sufficient

We expect

He'll pull something from up his sleeve you'll see
It'll end with a bang, the big finale
It's not over till the fat lady sings

He'll have held something special back
Always save the best till last
Wait for the fireworks, there's bound to be fireworks

I'm stood at the door again
having said all I've got to say, having had a great time
nervous that I could spoil it all in 3 seconds

Am I the only one who feels
there's too much onus on the notion of climax
Am I lacking in stamina, character, goodwill

Are people so fickle
that the last thing you say colours every other gesture?

Are people's memories so short they cannot cast their
	minds back
to five or ten minutes before the end?

I can never kiss that much more
than I kissed at the height of my passion.

I can never wave that better wave
exert that extra effort
surpass everything that's gone before

So a thank you and goodnight will have to suffice

Of course
if I do happen to make a grand exit
two minutes later I have to return
having forgotten my hat

A Prayer For the Hesitant

A pale blue dot
amid a family portrait

This is your home planet
you are where you were born to be
breathe

The world is your living room
you are almost friends
your ancestors, your family and
over ten thousand saints look down

Nobody means you any harm
not even God or nature
you can choose not to fear

The universe expects nothing
Every single thing is more than nothing
You have already exceeded expectation

If you forget me
my name
this moment
remember only this
you are good enough

imperfect as we are
you are good enough

A Message to my Species

I will not live on
my son will be the last of me
my evolutionary line is going out in a blaze of indifference

I quite like that
our little joke on the selfish gene
our snub to the scramble
for permanence and immortality

The rest of the universe will just have to get on
without me and my family
and our genetic material

This is the summit of our possibility
the culmination of millions of years' preparation
a wondrous cascade of consequence
a glorious accident embraced

Thank you life
thank you universe
we'll have the best time we can

then you are on your own
try not to fuck it up